National Recreation Area

GUIDE TO BOATING

PLACES TO GO AND THINGS TO SEE AND DO

Geoffrey Schneider
and
Rose Houk

Southwest Parks and Monuments Association
Tucson, Arizona

Library of Congress Cataloging-in-Publication Data

Schneider, Geoffrey.
    Lake Mead National Recreation Area guide to boating : places to go and things to see and do / written by Geoffrey Schneider and Rose Houk.
        p.   cm.
    ISBN 1-877856-78-9
    1. Boats and boating—Lake Mead National Recreation Area (Ariz. and Nev.)—Guidebooks.   2. Lake Mead National Recreation Area (Ariz. and Nev.)—Guidebooks. I. Houk, Rose, 1950-   .   II. Title.
GV776.L35S36   1997
                                        97-32496
                                            CIP

Published by Southwest Parks and Monuments Association
221 N. Court
Tucson, Arizona 85701

Net proceeds from SPMA publications support educational and research programs in the National Park Service.

Editorial by Derek Gallagher
Design by Hespenheide Design
Maps by The DLF Group
Photography by Michael Collier except as follows: Bud Nielsen, front cover *motor yacht;* Larry Ulrich, front cover, *beavertail cactus blooms,* pages 22–23, 41, 42; Gary Kramer, page 13, *desert bighorn sheep;* Lawerence Parent, pages 26, 28–29, *bottom and right.*

Illustrations by Mary Hirsch, page 16 and *razorback sucker* on page 52; Kent Pendleton courtesy of the Colorado Division of Wildlife, pages 52–53.

♲ Printed on recycled paper with inks from renewable resources

	Food service
	Boat permitted
	Fishing permitted
P	Boat trailer parking
	Restrooms
	Store
	Ranger station
	Marina
	Lodging
	Fuel
▲	Campground
	RV and trailer village
	Paved launch ramp

Look for these symbols to find which services are available at different places on the lakes.

CONTENTS

At dusk a peacefulness settles in. The wind softens, and the lake turns to satin. The stillness is broken only by the primeval calls of a small flock of Canada geese floating over, looking for a nighttime resting place, and a fish pirouetting out of the water snapping up supper. As night comes up over the desert, a full moon slides up in a cleft over the Black Mountains, bathing the desert valley in pearl light.

Whether you've been roaring up the lake all day in a fast jetboat, or sitting in a little skiff in a quiet cove angling for bass, there's no more magical time on the water than this edge between day and night. Lake Mead National Recreation Area weaves this kind of magic through all kinds of attractions based on water: boating, skiing, fishing, swimming, scuba diving, windsurfing, camping. The water is also the highway that leads to exploration of spectacular scenery, wildlife, botanical delights, unearthly geology, and deep, rich history.

Lake Mead National Recreation Area is big, it's diverse, and it's extreme. Here are a million and a half acres of land, ranging from the heights of Mount Dellenbaugh, at nearly 7,000 feet on the Shivwits Plateau, down to 500 feet above sea level at the south end of Lake Mohave. Temperatures can be harsh, from 120 degrees Fahrenheit in the desert in summer to well below freezing in winter on the high plateaus.

From the mouth of the Grand Canyon the park follows the Arizona-Nevada border along what was formerly 140 miles of the Colorado River. The two big lakes—Mead and Mohave—are the big draw here. Lake Mead, created

Lake Mohave sunrise

by the construction of Hoover Dam on the Colorado River, is the largest artificial lake in the country. Like a mirage in the desert, its deep blue waters shimmer amid the surrounding Mojave Desert. In sheer dimensions, Lake Mead is impressive: 110 miles long when the lake is full; 550 miles of shoreline; around 500 feet at greatest depth; 255 square miles of surface; and when filled to capacity, 28 million acre-feet of water, about two years' flow of the Colorado River. Sixty-seven-mile-long Lake Mohave, formed by Davis Dam, still retains in its upper reaches some of the character of the old Rio Colorado.

Hoover Dam, the first of a series of huge dams intended to harness the Colorado River, was built at the height of the Great Depression in the 1930s. As President Franklin D. Roosevelt dedicated it in 1935, the gates closed and Lake Mead started to fill. Construction began on Davis Dam in 1941 but was interrupted by World War II. Workers completed the dam in 1953. Both Hoover and Davis dams were built primarily for flood control, water storage, fulfillment of water commitments to Mexico, and power generation. The water-based recreation provided by the lakes, at first a sidelight, now attracts around ten million people every year.

Hoover Dam astride Black Canyon, which separates Lakes Mead and Mohave

The Land

Rolling back an imaginary film to the dimmest frames of earth's history, you can see rock in places in Lake Mead National Recreation Area that is about a billion and a half years old—old rock indeed. Advancing the film forward, say 500 to 250 million years ago, this was ocean instead of desert. The carbonates and marine life that settled to the bottom of the ocean were eventually compressed into thousands of feet of sedimentary rock. Fossils in lime-stones are evidence of this ancient marine world.

Millions of years of seas and mountains and deserts came and went, adding layer upon layer to the geologic story. Fast forwarding to about 22 million years ago, the earth started to buckle and heave. For 17 million years, this was an inhospitable place. Massive earthquakes ripped apart the land and boiling lava spewed forth from explosive volcanoes. This chaos shaped the stark, yet strikingly beautiful, landscape we see today—tilted, broken rock in rainbows of red and orange, white, gray, tan, brown, and subtle shades in between; isolated mountain ranges razor

Gale Hills

Iceberg Ridge

sharp on the horizon, cones of debris fanning out at their feet.

During this time, the earth's crust stretched and extended, forming the Basin and Range geologic province, which includes most of what is now Nevada and parts of western Arizona and western Utah. This area is appropriately named, for the topography beats out a rhythm of wide, downdropped basins, or valleys, separated by north-south trending mountain ranges. Left standing high to the east, relatively unscathed, was the Colorado Plateau. The Grand Wash Cliffs at the eastern edge of Lake Mead neatly mark the boundary between the Plateau and the Basin and Range.

A major feature of the entire region took shape about two to four million years ago. At that time, the Colorado River carved its present westerly course through the Grand Canyon and south to the Gulf of California.

Though the land assumed most of its present topography by then, even as recently as 12,000 years ago the climate was much different from what it is today. Under the influence of continental ice sheets to the north, conditions here were cooler and moister. Pine trees graced the hills, and mammoths and sloths lumbered around the countryside not far from what is now the glitterland of the Las Vegas Strip. Finally, about 11,000 years ago, with the retreat of the great ice sheets, the climate warmed and dried and the deserts formed. The Mojave Desert specifically has been created by the rain shadow cast by the Sierra Nevada and other mountains in southern California. The high ranges intercept moisture sweeping in from the Pacific Ocean, leaving the Mojave with a scant three to five inches of precipitation a year.

All the geologic forces of the past continue today. The landscape of Lake Mead is still being molded by water, wind, and movements in the earth, sometimes slowly and invisibly, other times suddenly and dramatically.

Looking to the northwest, a placid Lake Mohave

The Plants

The Mojave Desert is the hottest and driest on the continent, but it still holds a unique mosaic of native plant life. While the blistering heat sends people flocking to the cool waters of Lake Mead, the plants just sit there and take it. For them, this desert is home. They have "learned" to adapt to the heat, the meager, variable moisture, and the high rate of evaporation.

In some years, mild rains dampen the desert during the fall and winter months, and heavy downpours deluge the Mojave during summer monsoons. But drought, sometimes lasting for several years, is more the norm. Plants have survived here for long periods with no water at all.

The first image that flashes into most people's minds when they think about hardy desert plants is the cacti. While there's no shortage of these spiny dwellers in the recreation area, plant life here is as diverse and unique as the park itself. Despite this diversity, all the plants share a common trait: the ability to survive frequent droughts and extreme swings in temperature.

Plants have developed three basic ways to cope with what the desert dishes out. They escape, evade, or resist. One of the most wondrous shows on earth unfolds in the Mojave in the spring, after winter rains have blessed the desert. Then the usually drab hillsides and dry washes are transformed into opulent carpets of white, yellow, pink, and purple flowers. These are the "annuals" that escape drought by sprouting, blooming, and setting seed in one brief season. In years when conditions are not so good, their seeds remain dormant in the soil. Annuals are often small plants with colorful, sweet-scented flowers that

Left to right: 1 Indian paintbrush, 2 beavertail cactus, 3 Joshua trees, 4 rock nettle, 5 prince's plume, 6 desert tobacco, 7 desert fir

attract bees and other insects that pollinate them. Desert star, gravel ghost, Fremont pincushion, phacelia, desert verbena, and the common forget-me-not decorate the recreation area.

A second group of plants—the drought evaders— has learned to deal with the searing heat and prolonged dry periods by reducing life functions to a bare minimum. They may look dead, but they are very much alive, simply awaiting resurrection that will inevitably come with the next rains. Then, seemingly overnight, they will sprout leaves and sometimes flowers too. A good example of a drought evader is the ocotillo, a plant of the Sonoran Desert that extends into the southern end of the recreation area. This tall, many-branched shrub has an extensive root system just beneath the ground that takes immediate advantage of any rain. Often the ocotillo lacks leaves, which helps it conserve water by limiting the amount of surface area exposed to the sun. But when rain comes, fresh green leaves sprout nearly instantaneously.

The third group—the drought resistors—includes a wide variety of shrubs and woody plants. Members of the cactus family are superlative drought

resistors, employing several techniques. Cacti have mostly done away with water-wasting leaves and instead photosynthesize through their green stems. The stems have a waxy coating that reduces water loss. Some cacti have massive root systems to extract as much water as possible from the soil and carry them through dry times; they can also sprout temporary "rain roots" whenever moisture comes their way. Some cacti have mastered the art of vegetative reproduction. The spiny joints drop to the ground and take root on the spot. Witness the amazing concentration of teddybear chollas along the road into Cottonwood on Lake Mohave. All cacti are perennials, surviving from one year to the next, adding new growth as conditions permit.

A most remarkable plant of the Lake Mead area is the Joshua tree. This yucca, trademark of the Mojave Desert, can grow to a height of twenty feet or more. Joshua trees live where moisture is a little more plentiful, between 3,500 to 5,000 feet in elevation. In good years,

Joshua tree at Meadview

they bear thick clusters of waxy white flowers on the tips of their gangly arms. Boaters heading out the Meadview Road toward South Cove and Pearce Ferry pass an extraordinary forest of wise-looking Joshua trees. A shorter, stouter relative of the Joshua tree, the Mojave yucca, sports long, daggerlike leaves.

The most common, but often overlooked, shrub in the park is the creosote bush, an ably adapted drought resistor. The shiny olive-green leaves appear to be wet, but that sheen comes from a resinous coating that prevents moisture loss and imparts a rich odor to creosote bush. In spring these limber-branched bushes—carefully spaced over lakeside alluvial fans—dance with lemon-yellow flowers that turn to silvery furred seedpods. White bursage, a companion shrub, is nearly as common as creosote bush at the lowest elevations.

A walk up a side canyon may yield a real surprise— verdant springs flowing forth from the ground, some of them warm to hot. These springs, at least forty of them in the park, are unique spots of greenery, with desert willows, mesquites, and other water-loving plants, including the non-native tamarisk.

The Animals

All kinds of wildlife thrive in the land, air, and waters of Lake Mead National Recreation Area. The lakes, in particular, are a major habitat for birds and hundreds of species of native mammals, reptiles, amphibians, fish, and insects.

Lake Mead and Lake Mohave provide places where waterfowl can rest and renew their strength during their fall and spring migrations. You'll see cormorants, grebes, coots, teals, ducks, and geese by the tens of thousands, some migrants, some residents. Often, boaters will spy a solitary great blue heron standing among the reeds, straight and tall as the reeds themselves, alert, silent, and well camouflaged. When a heron takes wing, it is like a prehistoric pterodactyl.

During the winter a small number of eagles, both balds and goldens, find a haven here. These big raptors don't typically nest in the park, but keep a keen eye out and you may spot a white-capped bald eagle soaring above the lakes or hills, talons primed for a fish, ground squirrel, or jackrabbit. Endangered peregrine falcons pass through on their migrations from Canada to South America. Encouragingly, a few peregrine pairs have taken up nesting on high cliffs within the park during spring and early summer. Said to be the fastest birds on earth, peregrines can dive at speeds up to 200 miles an hour.

Songbirds such as orioles, flycatchers, and warblers are of interest these days. Known as "neotropical migrants," these birds travel all the way from the rainforests of Central

Desert Bighorn Sheep
Left: Great egret near Willow Beach

Regal horned lizard
Background: Patch-nose snake

and South America to nest and raise their young in the United States and Canada. With deforestation and other human activities increasingly affecting their habitat, places like Lake Mead, where these birds stop over and breed, are gaining in importance.

The existence of another small bird—the glossy, black phainopepla—hinges on the continued protection mesquite trees receive in the recreation area. The bird's main food is the berries of the parasitic mistletoe that grows on mesquites. And in a mutually beneficial relationship, phainopeplas help fertilize mesquites with their droppings.

One of the finest wildlife sightings for recreationists is a glimpse of bighorn sheep grazing on the slopes or drinking at water's edge. The rams are distinguished by massive, spiral horns. They seem to sense how majestic they are, striking supremely elegant poses on the cliff sides. Ewes and lambs have smaller horns that do not form the great curls of the mature males.

Like all native creatures here, desert bighorn have adapted to this world. They negotiate the rocky terrain with surprising speed and agility, escaping predators such as mountain lions. Bighorns' bodies are designed to minimize water loss, and if necessary they can go several days without drinking.

Bighorn sheep live in matriarchal societies. A dominant female leads a herd, which for much of the year consists primarily of ewes and their lambs. The rams tend to stay together in bachelor groups until the summer breeding season. It is then that the sharp crack of their horns reverberates as they engage in the serious game of head butting to establish dominance and attract prospective mates. The rams are well armored for this ritual, so injuries are rare.

The bighorn population in the park is doing quite well. Wildlife managers transplant animals from herds here to other parts of the western United States.

Another large mammal seen in much fewer numbers than bighorn is the mule deer. Most of these long-eared, white-rumped deer inhabit the higher plateaus and mountains on the eastern edge of the recreation area. A few mountain lions do live within the park, mostly in the mountain ranges, but sightings are rare. Coyotes, kit foxes, badgers, and bobcats are fairly common.

Most boaters and campers have heard the forlorn "hee-haw" braying of wild burros. Not native to the area, these burros are the offspring of animals that escaped or were turned loose by miners and ranchers. The Park Service is removing them because they cause severe soil erosion, damage plants, and compete with native animals.

This is desert country, ideal for reptiles. Several kinds of snakes, lizards, and even a species of tortoise live here. The black and white California kingsnake, coachwhip, garter snake, and glossy snake inhabit the park. Several varieties of poisonous pit vipers, or rattlesnakes, call this home as well. They include Mojave green, diamondback, speckled, and sidewinder rattlesnakes.

Lizards are a regular feature. Chuckwallas are relatively abundant and can reach good size, a foot or more in length. You may see one basking on a cliff, but if this shy vegetarian senses a threat, it wedges into a rock crevice, inflates its body with air, and can't be dislodged. Other lizards darting from rock to shrub include the horned, collared, desert spiny, desert iguana, western fence, whiptail, and zebra-tailed.

A land-based turtle, the desert tortoise, also calls the Mojave Desert home. Though you may not often see this slow, lumbering tortoise, look for the half-moon-shaped burrows it digs in the banks of washes or on gravel slopes. Husky, elephant-like legs, rough gray skin, and a patchwork pattern on the shell are the tortoise's distinguishing characteristics. The hard shell protects the tortoise from predators and prevents moisture loss; in addition, the desert tortoise has a built-in reservoir of water in its large bladder. Desert tortoises have adapted to their arid home with this gift for conserving water, spending much of their life underground. They also enjoy a long life in which to reproduce (tortoises live sixty to one hundred years). But the Mojave Desert population of desert tortoises is threatened now by a virulent respiratory disease, captures and shootings, and loss of habitat. Fortunately in the environs around Lake Mead, their habitat is protected and their numbers are healthy.

The Fish

Several fish native to the Colorado River system have suffered severe declines because of damming of the free-flowing, silt-laden, warm river. Only a few humpback chubs, bonytail chubs, and Colorado squawfish (once called "white salmon") have been found in the lakes. Lake Mohave still contains the largest remaining population of one species, the razorback sucker, but the fish's future is precarious.

Meanwhile, non-native game fish have been doing fine. Not long after Lakes Mead and Mohave were created, game fish were introduced into their waters. Today, a multimillion-dollar sport fishing industry provides countless hours of recreation for boaters and shore anglers alike.

As soon as Lake Mead began to fill, fishing enthusiasts introduced largemouth bass to the lake, now the premier sport fish. Each year this renowned species attracts professional fishing tournaments to both Lakes Mead and Mohave.

In 1969 game managers first introduced striped bass into Lake Mead, and stocking continued in the early 1970s. Since then, stripers have become another coveted game fish in both lakes.

Rainbow trout are also stocked in both lakes and make up a significant portion of the catch, particularly in the winter months. You can also fish for channel catfish, black crappie, green sunfish, bluegill, and carp. Crayfish and threadfin shad, an introduced bait fish, are the main food of these game fish.

Top to bottom: Bonytail, Black Crappie, Bluefish, and Striped Bass

Native Americans

Ice-age hunters may have appeared in the Lake Mead area about 12,000 years ago, stalking mammoths and other big game animals. As the glaciers retreated and the big animals became extinct, hunters turned their attention to mule deer, bighorn sheep, and smaller quarry such as rabbits, rodents, and birds. Wild plants gained in importance as food. In their constant search for something to eat, these people migrated with the seasons. From spring through summer, they stayed in the lowlands harvesting yucca and cactus fruits. In autumn they ventured to nearby mountains to gather pine nuts and hunt deer. Because of their nomadic existence, these people left little in the way of permanent evidence of their lives.

But by about 2,000 years ago, there is substantial evidence of people living within the bounds of the recreation area. Population concentrated in the lower reaches of the Muddy and Virgin rivers, where the people at first lived in pithouse villages. Their skill at weaving willow and yucca fibers into baskets and mats is legendary. Around A.D. 700, they were starting to build aboveground mud and stone dwellings all along the Muddy, including the excavated site called Pueblo Grande de Nevada, or Lost City, at the north end of the Overton Arm of Lake Mead.

They became adept farmers and for more than a thousand years raised corn, squash, beans, and cotton along the rivers. They also continued hunting bighorn sheep and rabbits, along with gathering a host of wild plants, including mesquite beans, yucca fruit, and gourds.

Petroglyphs in Grapevine Canyon

They mined salt along the Virgin River and wove cotton into fine cloth.

The discovery of ocean shells in Pueblo settlements indicates they had contact with people from the Gulf of California. They may have exchanged local turquoise for the shell and exotic pottery. Willow Beach on Lake Mohave was an important trading center. In places, often along watercourses, they left signs of their passage in the form of petroglyphs—drawing and etchings on rock faces of animal and human forms and intriguing geometric and abstract designs.

You'll come across Petroglyphs in various parts of the recreation area. These fragile reminders of the past depend on your care to preserve them for future generations.

About 850 years ago these native Americans suddenly left the area or radically changed their lifestyle. The reasons are speculation. Was there prolonged drought? Did their intensive farming deplete the soil's productivity? Was there some kind of internal upheaval? Or did they have conflicts with new arrivals to the area, such as the Southern Paiute?

The Southern Paiute entered the region around A.D. 1000. They survived by staying on the move and exercising well-honed skills as hunters of small game and foragers of plant foods. Though they knew their environment intimately, there were undeniably lean times. Bands of Southern Paiute were living and farming small plots in the Lake Mead area when Euro-Americans first arrived. Yuman-speaking groups were in the region, too. The Mohave and Maricopa farmed and fished along the lower Colorado River, while the Hualapai and Havasupai claimed territory over a huge portion of western Arizona. The descendants of these native Americans still live in the Lake Mead area today.

Euro-Americans

The first white man who left a written record of entering the area was intrepid explorer Jedediah Smith. In 1826, he and a small band of trappers came down along the Virgin River and through Black Canyon on their way to California. Smith went into the prehistoric salt mines and wrote of Indians farming along the river.

In 1858, two rival steamboats, the *Explorer* and the *General Jesup,* made their way up the Colorado River from Yuma into Black Canyon. Until 1909, steamboats continued traveling upstream, bringing men and supplies to mining districts such as Searchlight, Eldorado, Gold Butte, and Katherine. On the return trip to the Gulf of California, the boats were laden with gold and other ore from the mines. Throughout the recreation area, mine shafts and equipment stand idle and rusty, left from the hurly-burly days when mining was king.

During the mid 1860s another group arrived, intending to stay. In 1864, Brigham Young, head of the Church of Jesus Christ of Latter-day Saints, sent Anson Call to set up a trading center on the north side of the Colorado River. Callville provided an outlet for Utah freight for a few years. Later, more Mormons were sent on a mission to set up permanent settlements along the Muddy River. They did so, founding the towns of Saint Thomas, Kaolin, and Overton (only Overton remains high and dry).

With a boat as your magic carpet, you can follow that highway of water to all kinds of places in Lake Mead National Recreation Area—historic places in one of the last explored areas in the country, inhabited by people who knew well the ways of the river and the desert. You can see a geologic display like none other on earth, watch the shore for signs of birdlife, wonder at the clever adaptations of a desert shrub, splash in the cool water, or wet a line and hope those stripers are taking what you're offering.

Bass fishing near Beehive Island

CAN BUOYS
Green color—odd numbers—indicates left side of safe channel when headed up-lake away from dam.

DAYMARK
Green Square—odd numbers—on left shore when headed up-lake away from dam.

NUN BUOYS
Red color—even numbers—indicates right side of safe channel when headed up-lake away from dam.

DAYMARK
Red Triangle—even numbers—on right shore when headed up-lake away from dam.

MID-CHANNEL
Red and white—no numbers—pass these buoys safely to either side.

OBSTRUCTION
Marker—do not pass between buoy and shore.

BOATING GUIDE

This guide uses Hoover Dam as the base point. Mileages in the text appear in ascending order upstream from the dam on Lake Mead, and in descending order downstream from the dam on Lake Mohave.

Visitors cruise both lakes on all manner of craft—powerboats, fishing boats, runabouts, sailboats, patio boats, houseboats, canoes, and kayaks. Canoeists, kayakers, and oar-powered boaters will find the smaller bays and coves and narrower reaches more to their liking. You can rent boats at some marinas or take a concessionaire-run paddle cruise or raft trip. Water skiers and swimmers enjoy warm, clear waters many months of the year, and you'll discover pleasant swimming locations at places like Boulder Beach. Windsurfers can take advantage of the winds, which frequently blow with considerable strength. You can moor your boat and take off for a hike up a side canyon or dry wash. Or, you might just want to set up a lawn chair on a sandy beach, dangle your feet in the water, and watch a magnificent sunset.

Boating Regulations and Etiquette

The "Rules of the Road" of boating apply on the lakes, and boaters need to learn marker and buoy signs. Have good nautical charts and maps, know distress signals, take proper safety equipment, and leave a float plan with someone before you launch.

Weather can change without warning on the lakes, and winds are a force to be dealt with. Should you find yourself unexpectedly in unsafe conditions, you will be better off waiting in a sheltered cove rather than trying to outrun the weather. Before launching, check for red storm warning flags posted at developed marinas when wind conditions warrant. White strobe lights blinking on shore indicate winds in excess of seventeen miles per hour, and boaters should seek shelter. For a recording of current wind speeds, call posted telephone numbers for Wind Talker.

For more information, pick up a free boater's packet at any ranger station in the recreation area.

Exploring off the Water

Take plenty of water with you on hikes, and start drinking it before you feel thirsty. Rain does fall here sometimes, so choose camps with care—what may be a dry wash now may not stay dry in a storm. Pack out all trash, and leave your campsite cleaner than you found it. This is home to the plants, animals, and rocks, so please respect them. Likewise, do not deface petroglyphs or collect any artifacts. Also, desert soils are covered with a delicate crust that takes centuries to recover from trampling.

When visiting hot springs, be aware that an amoeba may live in the water that can cause a rare infection and possible death. Avoid immersing your nose or head in the hot pools.

Fishing Licenses

Information about fishing seasons, catch limits, and license requirements is available from the Arizona Department of Game and Fish and the Nevada Division of Wildlife. Fishing licenses are sold at all marinas in the recreation area and at most bait and tackle shops and sporting goods stores in Las Vegas, Boulder City, Laughlin, Bullhead City, Kingman, and Overton.

CIRCLES mark controlled areas. Use caution.

DIAMOND shape warns of danger. Nature of danger may be indicated inside the diamond.

DIAMOND shape with cross. Boats keep out.

SQUARE or RECTANGLE gives information, names, distance.

DIVERS FLAG means divers are submerged. Stay clear.

STORM WARNING FLAGS AND LIGHTS

Flags   Lights

Small Craft Advisory

Gale Warning

Storm Warning

LAKE MEAD

The Lake Mead portion of this guide is organized in six sections: Boulder Basin, Virgin Basin, Overton Arm, Temple Basin, Gregg Basin, and Upper Lake Mead. You can also drive to various parts of the lake along the Lakeshore and Northshore roads.

Boulder Basin

The most heavily visited basin on the lake is Boulder Basin. Close to Las Vegas, it attracts that growing city's residents and millions of visitors as well.

Because of Boulder Basin's popularity, you'll find more visitor services in and around it than at any of the other basins. These include three full-service marinas with boat launch ramps, two additional paved launch ramps with adjacent restroom facilities, four campgrounds, a lodge, three National Park Service ranger stations, and the Alan Bible Visitor Center.

Las Vegas Bay, on the northwest side of Boulder Basin, is the part of the lake nearest Las Vegas. This large bay contains Las Vegas Bay Marina, Government Wash launch ramp, and the popular fishing areas of Gypsum Wash and Las Vegas Wash.

Las Vegas Wash was originally a stream fed by natural artesian springs originating in the Las Vegas Valley. Mexican traders along the Old Spanish Trail found this stream in the 1840s and followed it to its source. From the luxuriant vegetation surrounding the springs, they named the valley Las Vegas, which means "the meadows."

Now the wash flows into Lake Mead year-round with the city's treated sewage effluent and other runoff.

Lake Mead Marina is on the southwest side of Boulder Basin. Entering and departing the marina, boaters will notice a large white metal structure at the south end of Saddle Island. Like a giant mosquito, this water intake tower dips deep into Lake Mead to draw out water

SERVICES AT
Lake Mead Marina

The Alan Bible Visitor Center at Lake Mead

for use in Henderson, Nevada, and for the Nevada Division of Wildlife's Lake Mead Hatchery. Several times a month from late fall through early spring, rainbow trout reared at the hatchery are stocked here. The facility rears several hundred thousand trout each year for stocking not only at Lake Mead, but also Lake Mohave and other public fishing waters in southern Nevada. Two submerged intakes on the east side of Saddle Island withdraw more than three-fourths of Las Vegas's water supply.

Immediately south of Lake Mead Marina are Boulder Beach and Hemenway Harbor. The entire beachfront

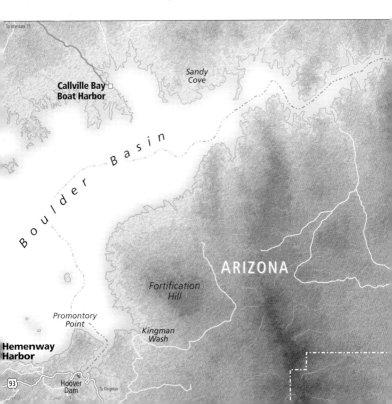

Lake Mead Marina at Boulder Beach

is zoned for specific uses, including swimming, personal watercraft, skiing, and special events.

From the large volume of boat traffic, it's easy to see that Hoover Dam is a popular attraction. Launching at any of the Boulder Basin ramps, you pass a series of five or six islands—Pyramid, Big Boulder, Middle Boulder, Little Boulder, Rock Island, and Deadman's Island, all of them not always visible at high water. From there, you swing around the nose of Promontory Point and enter the head of Black Canyon. Before you is a closeup view of the upstream side of Hoover Dam—1,244 feet long at the crest—the four intake towers, spillways on the Arizona and Nevada sides of

SERVICES AT
Boulder Beach and Hemenway Harbor

Hoover Dam intake towers with Visitor Center in background

the lake, and the Hoover Dam Visitor Center. On the Arizona side, look for a "pillbox," a gun emplacement overlooking Hoover Dam. It was built and staffed by the military during World War II to protect the dam from saboteurs.

Turning now and heading uplake, the tall mesa dominating the skyline on the south side of the lake is Fortification Hill. Its cap and drapings of black are a succession of more than a hundred lava flows that emerged from deep inside the earth approximately six to twelve million years ago. At the base of Fortification Hill are mounds of colorful hills called the Paint Pots, good landmarks. Their bright crimson color is due to oxidation—or "rusting"—of the rocks. A graded dirt road leads down Kingman Wash at the base of Fortification Hill, a well-used put-in spot for boats though also a path of major summer floods.

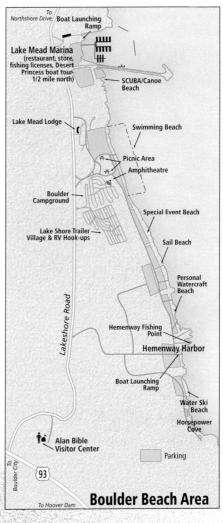

To Northshore Drive · Boat Launching Ramp

Lake Mead Marina (restaurant, store, fishing licenses, Desert Princess boat tour- 1/2 mile north)

SCUBA/Canoe Beach

Lake Mead Lodge

Swimming Beach

Picnic Area
Amphitheatre

Boulder Campground

Special Event Beach

Lake Shore Trailer Village & RV Hook-ups

Sail Beach

Personal Watercraft Beach

Lakeshore Road

Hemenway Fishing Point

Hemenway Harbor

Boat Launching Ramp

Water Ski Beach

Horsepower Cove

Alan Bible Visitor Center

To Boulder City

93

Parking

To Hoover Dam

Boulder Beach Area

Paint Pots near Kingman Wash

SERVICES AT
Callville Bay Marina

The high Muddy Mountains stand on the northern horizon, with Black Mesa in the foreground. At their base is Callville Bay Marina (**MILE ⑩**). It's about a five-mile fetch of open water across Boulder Basin to reach the marina.

Callville, also called Fort Call, was a remote Mormon shipping center established in 1864 by namesake Anson Call. It was the final point of

Lake Mead from Boulder Beach

navigation for steamboats coming up the Colorado River. With completion of the transcontinental railroad farther north in Utah in 1869, Callville's days as a major shipping point were numbered. The foundations of the stone warehouses are now deep under the water of Lake Mead.

Sandy Cove, two miles east of Callville Bay, is aptly named for its inviting sandy beach, rare on Lake Mead. This is a popular spot for sunbathing, picnicking, and swimming and is recommended for houseboat mooring.

Another favored stop, Wishing Well Cove, is situated on the south side of Boulder Basin in Boulder Canyon. This sheer-walled, narrow, winding cove is an inspiring place.

Boulder Canyon's narrow granite walls separate Boulder Basin from Virgin Basin. Boulder Canyon was the first site investigated for a dam, explaining why Hoover Dam was originally called Boulder Dam (even though it was built in Black Canyon).

Herds of desert bighorn sheep inhabit both shores of Boulder Basin. Watch for their silhouettes on the skyline. You can also see them scampering down the rocks to drink from the lake.

Fortification Hill

Virgin Basin

At Boulder Wash Cove **(MILE ⑲)** the lake's huge Virgin Basin opens up, with fascinating displays of geology flanking every side. Because of its relative isolation, Virgin Basin

Springtime lupines near Fortification Hill

has no marinas or other services. Boulder Wash Cove, fairly protected, is popular for boating and camping. Boulder Wash features a considerable variety of plant and animal life, a good place to hike and take photographs. Fishing for striped bass and channel catfish can also be good here from April through November. Continuing east along the north shoreline are the Little Gyp Beds, Debbie's Cove, and Boathouse Cove.

Across the basin, on the south side, are Petroglyph Bay and Petroglyph Wash. Although we don't know the

Virgin Basin with the Black Mountains in the foreground

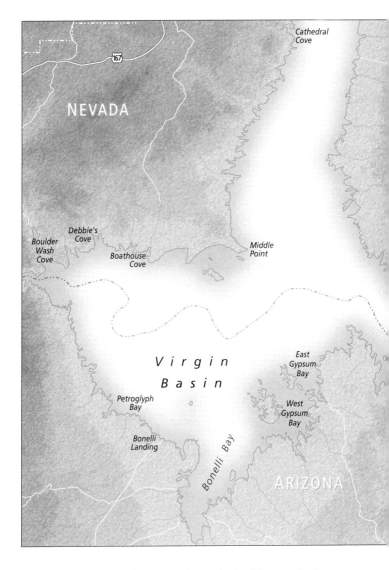

exact meanings, etchings on the rocks in this area depict humans, animals, and an array of abstract and geometric designs crafted by earlier native Americans. Please take care not to damage these fragile remnants of the past.

Continuing up the Virgin Basin on the same side is Bonelli Bay. This large bay, fed by Detrital Wash which heads near Kingman, Arizona, receives significant runoff during major rainstorms. An unimproved launch area at Bonelli is the only public facility of any size in the Virgin Basin.

In the late 1800s, Daniel Bonelli established a ferry at the confluence of the Virgin and Colorado Rivers. From his farms at Saint Thomas and Rioville, he ferried salt, hay, and produce across to the south bank of the river. There

Above: High aerial view of the Gypsum Reefs
Right: Bonelli landing

the goods were freighted by wagons up Detrital Wash and over the Black Mountains, where they were again transferred to boats and taken across to the mines at Eldorado.

Northeast of Bonelli Bay, still on the south side heading toward Temple Basin, boaters will find East Gypsum Bay and West Gypsum Bay. Often referred to as the "Gyp Beds," the soil here has a heavy gypsum content. Gypsum is an evaporate, a shiny, whitish mineral that precipitated out of standing water in an ancient lakebed. The light-colored Gyp Beds erode into interesting patterns and host plants like bearpaw poppy and desert holly that actually prefer this soil. This is a good area for exploring in canoes and kayaks.

Overton Arm

North from the Virgin Basin, boaters enter twenty-five-mile-long Overton Arm, largest of Lake Mead's basins. On the west shore at the entry to Overton Arm is a spit of land called Middle Point (**MILE 25**), commemorating the historic confluence of the Virgin and Colorado Rivers.

The Virgin River originates in Utah and flows through Arizona and into Nevada on its route to Lake Mead. The Muddy River also comes into Overton Arm. It surfaces in springs about thirty miles north of the lake around Warm Springs, Nevada. During its brief run to Lake Mead, the Muddy River waters the rich agricultural lands of the Moapa Valley.

**SERVICES AT
Echo Bay**

Callville Bay Marina

There are two marinas on Overton Arm—Echo Bay and Overton Beach, both on the west shore.

On the east shore of Overton Arm, and from Echo Bay south on the west shore, boaters will find an abundance of coves and plenty of sandy beaches for camping. Best of all, not many people come to this part of the lake, so you'll enjoy plenty of space and solitude.

The badlands landscape is starkly beautiful. The rocks, many spewed from volcanoes millions of years ago, are as coarse as sandpaper and colored in crimson, black,

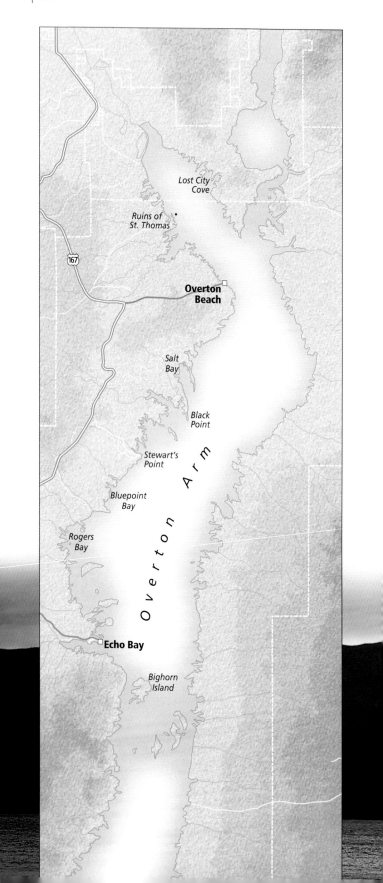

Lost City
Cove

Ruins of
St. Thomas

167

**Overton
Beach**

Salt
Bay

Black
Point

Stewart's
Point

Overton Arm

Bluepoint
Bay

Rogers
Bay

Echo Bay

Bighorn
Island

turquoise, and gray. They are soft rocks with little plant cover, and the steep slopes erode in a hurry.

Mountain ranges line both sides of Overton Arm. To the west are the Black and Muddy Mountains while Gold Butte and the Virgin Mountains rise to the east. Gold Butte is composed of rocks that date back 1.5 billion years, the oldest in the recreation area.

At first sight, the lower elevations appear to be covered only with creosote bush. But a closer look reveals beavertail and barrel cactus, bearpaw poppy, rabbitbrush, desert marigolds, Mojave yucca, mistletoe, and abundant stands of mesquite. When it blooms in spring, the beavertail's outrageous fuchsia flowers seem to mock the monotones of the landscape. The lovely bearpaw poppy is named for the clutch of furry, paw-shaped leaves at the base of the stem. This gypsum-and alkali-lover is a rare plant, growing only in a few places where its preferred soil type is available. The bearpaw poppy's delicate yellow flowers bloom at the tip of long slender stalks.

The Northshore Road (Route 167) affords access to the west side of Overton Arm. Along the way motorists see stupendous scenery and can stop to fish, hike, camp, and picnic on this part of the lake.

SERVICES AT
Overton Beach

Beavertail opuntia, with its bright flowers and spineless pads

South Virgin Mountains across from Echo Bay

Northshore Scenic Drive cuts through the Black Mountains

On the water, eight miles up the west shore of Overton Arm is Cathedral Cove, which sees heavy boater use. Towering walls surround the cove, and there's a small beach area. Watch for rocks just beneath the surface as you enter the cove.

Ten miles up, Bighorn Island rises out of the lake. Its name comes from the days when Lake Mead was filling in the 1930s and 1940s. As with all the "islands" in Lake Mead, Bighorn is not a true island but a butte attached to the mainland that the rising lake waters surrounded. On this particular "island," a bighorn ram became stranded, and the story goes that some people, concerned about his loneliness, saw that a few ewes were transported onto the island to keep him company. There are no bighorns on the island today.

A few miles up from Bighorn Island are Rogers Bay and Bluepoint Bay. These bays are named for warm springs that originate nearby. The streams that lead to the springs are interesting, rare wetland communities.

Stewart's Point, between Echo Bay and Overton Beach, is developed with private housing. Here and to the north, especially at Fire Cove and along the bar reefs off Black Point and Salt Bay, fishing for bass and stripers is said to be good.

Salt Bay and Salt Cove are named for plugs of salt (the common table variety) that have wedged up to the surface. The salts concentrated where old lakebeds evaporated. They were once buried but actually "flowed" to the surface. Both prehistoric and historic people have mined this salt.

Above Overton Beach on the west shore, the ruins of the town of Saint Thomas are under the waters of the lake. Saint Thomas was the town that never said die. Mormon hopefuls founded it in 1865 and were soon producing melons, almonds, wheat, beans, asparagus, grapes, and all kinds of berries and fruit. But in only five years, difficulties caused the residents of Saint Thomas to abandon their mission. Saint Thomas was resettled again in 1877, this time until the waters of Lake Mead began to lap at its foundations in the 1930s. As historians tell it, "the postmaster then hurled the cancellation stamp from the post office window," and the village of Saint Thomas was abandoned for the last time.

A thousand years earlier, other people lived along the Muddy River in what is now upper Overton Arm. At Lost City Cove, on the shore opposite the Saint Thomas ruins, the walls of prehistoric pueblos may be seen when the lake level is low. One of several Ancestral Puebloan

A houseboat moored in Cathedral Cove

villages, Lost City was excavated hurriedly as Lake Mead filled. Lost City Museum in the town of Overton, Nevada now displays some artifacts from the site.

In the highest reaches of Overton Arm, nourished by the Muddy River, is the Overton Wildlife Management Area, a great birdwatching spot. There are Canada geese, a number of species of ducks, and many shorebirds, as well as hawks, ravens, roadrunners, pheasants, and wild turkeys. If you're lucky, you may get to observe the antics of the perky top-notched Gambel's quail. It's also a great place to picnic.

Temple Basin

Separating Virgin Basin from Virgin Canyon is small, scenic Temple Basin. Entering the basin, you pass Boat Wreck Point (around MILE ㉜), and a couple of miles farther up on the north shore are sandstone hills descriptively named the Haystacks. For the next few miles, several coves

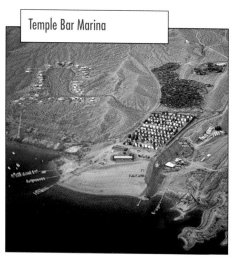

Temple Bar Marina

provide good anchorage and equally fine fishing.

Temple Bar Marina provides services in the area (MILE ㊱ on the south side). This is the last marina on the lake.

Across the lake from

Boat Wreck Point

NEVADA

Temple Basin

The Temple

Temple Bar Boat Harbor

ARIZONA

Gregg's Hideout

the marina rises a stunning sheer-walled rock formation called The Temple. Early explorers (some say Daniel Bonelli) named The Temple; it became a landmark for travelers along the Colorado River and remains one for boaters on Lake Mead. Geologists attribute its existence to a caprock of calcium carbonate that is hard as concrete. This cap protects The Temple from eroding away.

The south side of Temple Basin consists mainly of low hills, desert washes, and vast stretches of open land dominated by seemingly endless creosote bushes.

SERVICES AT

Temple Bar Marina

Temple Bar

Gregg Basin

At the head of Virgin Canyon and the entry to Gregg Basin is a place called Gregg's Hideout. William Grigg (common usage changed the spelling to "Gregg") had a ranch nearby and ran a paddleboat ferry across the Colorado River between Hualapai Wash and Sandy Point. At the ferry site in 1893, Utah cattleman Preston Nutter swam 5,000 reluctant steers across the river from Arizona and didn't lose a single animal.

Virgin Canyon's hard granite walls tower like a stone fortress from the waters of Lake Mead. In spring and early summer, scan these rocks for nesting golden eagles and prairie falcons. Anglers may have luck in the shaded areas along the canyon walls.

No marinas or other services are available in Gregg Basin. There is, however, a paved launch ramp along with restrooms and covered picnic tables at South Cove on the east side of the lake. You can reach this area by taking the Meadview turnoff on U.S. Highway 93. Sandy Point,

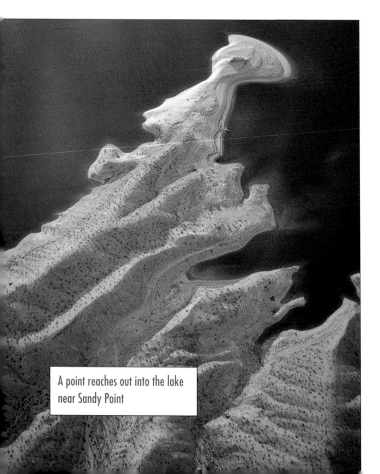

A point reaches out into the lake near Sandy Point

Mohave mound cactus above South Cove

located just north of South Cove, is a popular camping area for boaters. Fishing for channel catfish can be exceptional here from late spring through fall.

At **MILE 53** on the west shore is an area named Hell's Kitchen. It's highly appropriate, for the land is truly an inferno in the summer. With Gold Butte Mountain rising in Nevada and Grapevine Mesa in Arizona, this is a land of extremes. In winter, temperatures can plunge to below freezing while in summer this is one of the hottest places in North America.

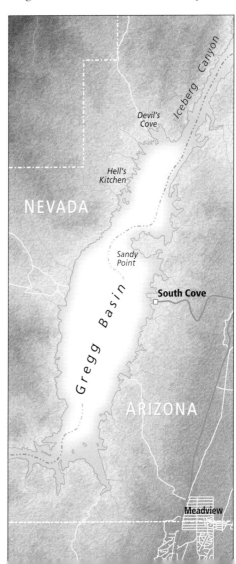

Iceberg Canyon

Devil's Cove

Hell's Kitchen

NEVADA

Sandy Point

Gregg Basin

South Cove

ARIZONA

Meadview

Upper Lake Mead

Iceberg Canyon in the upper reaches of Lake Mead presents exposures of old rock that has much more recently been tilted into dramatic chevrons by Basin-and-Range faulting. Just beyond Iceberg Canyon is the boundary line between Nevada and Arizona. East of this boundary, from MILE **58** on, Lake Mead is entirely within the state of Arizona.

Northeast of Iceberg Canyon, at MILE **60**, Grand Wash enters Lake Mead. On the northwest side of the wash is Lava Point, where erupting lava cooled into black basalt columns. Grand Wash Bay is a beautiful part of Lake Mead. Because it is so remote, it receives little boat traffic. This is as far as houseboats can go on the lake.

Rising east of Grand Wash Bay are the lofty Grand Wash Cliffs. A major structural feature, the Grand Wash Fault, is responsible for the magnificent 3,000-foot-high cliffs that run for a considerable distance north to south. The Grand Wash Cliffs mark the boundary between the two major geological provinces, the wildly tilted land of the Basin and Range and the flat-lying sediments of the Colorado Plateau.

Uplake from Grand Wash Bay is Grand Wash Canyon, and at MILE **61** is a bay called God's Pocket. Here

Grand Wash Cliffs from Pearce Ferry

Abandoned building at Pearce Ferry

the scenery begins to take on more of the aspect of the Grand Canyon.

Pearce Ferry (MILE **66**) is the last boat launch spot on Lake Mead. Like South Cove, motor vehicle access to Pearce Ferry is through Meadview, Arizona. Other than the unpaved launch ramp and primitive camping, no facilities are available in the area.

Here Harrison Pearce and his son John built and operated an oar-powered ferry. For about twenty years in the last century, they shuttled wagons and supplies back and forth on the Colorado.

Immediately uplake from Pearce Ferry, boaters enter Grand Canyon National Park. Shifting mudflats and sand bars, plus very dense vegetation that has grown up along the channel, make navigation much trickier. Depending on lake levels, the water can also be extremely shallow here.

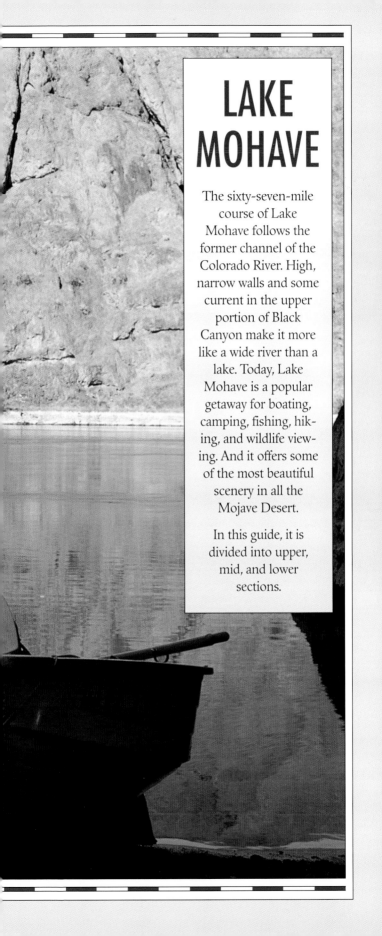

LAKE MOHAVE

The sixty-seven-mile course of Lake Mohave follows the former channel of the Colorado River. High, narrow walls and some current in the upper portion of Black Canyon make it more like a wide river than a lake. Today, Lake Mohave is a popular getaway for boating, camping, fishing, hiking, and wildlife viewing. And it offers some of the most beautiful scenery in all the Mojave Desert.

In this guide, it is divided into upper, mid, and lower sections.

Upper Lake

The upper twenty-five miles of Lake Mohave, stretching from the tailrace of Hoover Dam south to Eldorado Canyon, are enclosed by the dark volcanic rock of Black Canyon. It is at the head of Black Canyon that the 726-foot-high concrete plug of Hoover Dam was built, the largest dam in the Western Hemisphere.

With some river current to aid paddling, the Black Canyon stretch is popular among canoeists, who often put in just below the dam. (You'll need permission from the Bureau of Reclamation to put in on the Portal Road.) Boaters should be particularly wary when launching below the dam because of submerged rocks and reefs, rapids, and currents. Also, dam releases can cause water levels to fluc-

Eldorado Mountains above Lake Mohave

tuate as much as four to six vertical feet during the day, and upstream winds can make paddling a longer, harder chore. Canoeists must wear lifejackets for the first eleven miles through Black Canyon. Boats are prohibited from going upstream past the restriction cable several thousand yards below the dam.

The water coming immediately out of the depths of Lake Mead is cold—about fifty-three to fifty-five degrees Fahrenheit all year long. It warms up as you go downstream, though, and by Eldorado Canyon, swimming in summertime is pleasant.

But warm water is not far away in Black Canyon. Just after you launch, Gold-strike Canyon comes in on the west side. A short walk up the canyon leads to springs as hot as most people can stand. The hot springs pools and a water-fall festooned with emerald green algae are an inviting place to linger. You may want tennis shoes for the walk because the rocks in the stream are sharp; and remember not to submerge your head because of an infection-causing amoeba that may live in the water.

Three miles below the dam is Ringbolt Rapids, not really a "rapid" anymore except perhaps at very low water. About fifty yards above the rapids, on the east shore, an iron ringbolt is set in the rock. It is one of many such bolts installed by commercial steamboat crews in the 1860s to winch their vessels up through the rapids.

About a quarter mile below the rapids, on the east shore, is another fine soaking place—Arizona Hot Springs. About a quarter mile up the side canyon, you'll find a lower pool and a ladder reaching to an upper pool. The water cascades down a rock cliff and flows into a wash. About a mile more downstream, still more hot springs flow from the walls of Black Canyon. The furnace that heats these thermal springs to around 120 degrees Fahrenheit is molten rock in contact with groundwater, which makes its way to the surface along faults.

Colorado River below Ringbolt Rapids

Waterfall emptying into the Colorado River

Eastern shore of Lake Mohave, where it widens south of Cottonwood Cove

Keep your eyes peeled for bighorn sheep in Black Canyon. They perch improbably high up on the sheer cliffs, seemingly oblivious to the vertiginous dropoff below them.

Clinging to the west wall of the canyon a few miles farther down is an old gauging station used to monitor water and sediment levels while Hoover Dam was being built. The person tending the station crossed the river on a suspended cable car. Visible high up on the east bank is a trail and catwalk used by people doing the monitoring.

Approximately eleven miles below Hoover Dam is Willow Beach, a common takeout for Black Canyon boaters.

SERVICES AT

Willow Beach

Willow Beach is significant in Southwest prehistory as a long-standing trading center. Here archeologists found goods from eastern and central Arizona and from the Gulf of California, indicating an extended trade network between people of the Muddy and Virgin River country. Local people likely exchanged salt and turquoise for exotic pottery and shell.

Now Willow Beach (**MILE 52**) is the site of a U.S. Fish and Wildlife Service hatchery, which the public is welcome to visit. Besides rearing game fish for stocking in Lake Mohave, the hatchery is involved in a project to save the endangered razorback sucker. Lake Mohave contains the largest remaining population of these once-abundant native fish. But they are old fish, trapped in the lake after Davis Dam was completed. Young razorbacks are having trouble surviving predation. Biologists fear once the old ones die off there won't be any more razorback suckers. In a move to prevent this, they stage razorback

Campers north of Willow Beach

"roundups"; larvae are taken from the lake, held in hatchery raceways and rearing ponds for about six months, then released into the lake when they've attained a size that lets them avoid predators.

Below Willow Beach, the lake stretches for another three miles past steep, narrow canyon walls. Watch for the Monkey Hole, a fancifully named rock formation high on the east shore. Just above the Monkey Hole, on the same side, are petroglyphs that may represent the work of several tribes who camped along the Colorado River. These etchings have been here for hundreds to thousands of years and deserve our respect.

In the stretch called Windy Canyon and Copper Basin, Lake Mohave widens. Copper Basin offers several nice campsites at canyon mouths. Black Canyon ends at MILE ㊸. Near here, in March 1858, Lieutenant Joseph Christmas Ives's steamboat, the Explorer, hit a rock so hard it threw men over the bow and damaged the boat. Ives called the boulder Explorer Rock, and pronounced this the head of navigation for steamboats on the Colorado River. Later a few others winched steamboats and poled barges up another forty to fifty miles, to as far as Callville and the mouth of the Virgin River.

Four miles downstream Eldorado Canyon enters on the west side.

Mid Lake

In the mid-1800s, Eldorado Canyon was caught in the frenzy of a gold rush. The first claim, the Honest Miner, was filed here in 1859. The discovery of gold, and silver a couple of years later, led to the founding of a town of 1,500 souls on the west shore of the Colorado River. The steamboat business flourished, and barges brought drift-wood up from Cottonwood Island to fuel a custom stamp mill built at the mouth of Eldorado Canyon. But by the early part of the twentieth century, the rich veins of ore had played out and the mines closed. You can still see remnants of the mining activity at the nearby community of Nelson.

Even before Lake Mohave was created, Eldorado Canyon was the site of a small marina and a popular spot for anglers. In 1974, a flashflood scoured the canyon, destroyed the marina, and killed nine people. The marina and launch ramp were never rebuilt out of fear of future flooding.

Dunes at Cottonwood east, across from Cottonwood Point

In the Fire Mountain area (on the east side below Eldorado) elements of the Sonoran Desert begin to appear. Several plants and animals native to that desert live here, including the farthest north palo verde trees and Gila monsters. Beaded black and pink bands distinguish the venomous Gila monster from any other lizard. Because this is the northern edge of their range, a sighting is valuable knowledge for park biologists.

Aztec Wash, four miles below Eldorado Canyon on the west shore, offers good fishing

Owl Point Cove

Arizona Basin

ARIZONA

Cottonwood Cove

164

Cottonwood Basin

NEVADA

Cottonwood Island

for rainbow trout, channel catfish, and striped bass. Below Aztec Wash, on the same shore, a number of coves offer sandy beaches for good camps.

Another five miles or so to the south is Owl Point Cove, with some of the best fishing for striped bass. Chances are that anglers here are waiting for a striper to take their offerings of anchovies or squid. Anglers have pulled several stripers in excess of fifty pounds from Lake Mohave. Striped bass weren't known in this lake until after 1983. They likely came in over the Hoover Dam spillways. That record high-water year

Above: Rainbow Trout
Below: Razorback Sucker

forced use of the spillways for the first time in the dam's history.

Channel Catfish

SERVICES AT
Cottonwood Cove Marina

Between Owl Point and Cottonwood Cove is the open Arizona Basin, where coves provide protective habitat for young razorback suckers. This area also still contains thickets of native willows that resident beavers keep well thinned.

At the Cottonwood Cove Marina (MILE ㉒), boaters will find a paved launch ramp, restaurant, motel, convenience store, fuel, restrooms, and campgrounds, and a gaggle of ducks and gulls that form the official welcoming committee.

Cottonwood Cove wasn't always such a modern attraction. At the beginning of the century, it was a steamboat landing and site of a mill that produced gold bullion from ore mined at the nearby boom town of Searchlight.

Cottonwood Basin, located below Cottonwood Cove, is Lake Mohave's largest basin. It flooded Cottonwood Valley, where cottonwood trees once grew in abundance along the river. Before the lake was created, the Colorado separated here into two channels around Cottonwood Island, now under water.

Mallards below Hoover Dam

Lower Lake

The jagged, desolate Black Mountains extend on the east side and into California, while the Newberry Mountains preside on the west. Their highest peak, Spirit Mountain, rises to 5,639 feet. Its profile, like the horned head of a bison, is a constant presence on the horizon. Spirit Mountain is a special place to native Americans of the region. They call it Avi-Kwa-Ame, "the highest mountain," and say that at one time all the tribes lived there.

From the sublime to the silly, coves downstream on Lake Mohave have names like Chili Pepper and Sourdough. Princess Cove, on the east shore about six miles above Katherine Landing, is a new launch area with paved ramp, parking, and restrooms. Just south of Princess Cove is Gasoline Alley, with a deep, steep-walled canyon unusual on Lake Mohave.

Much of what is now the lower portion of Lake Mohave was once covered with the waters of Lake Chemehuevi. The Colorado River deposited sediments in this ice-age lake.

SERVICES AT

Lake Mohave Resort

Bighorn petroglyph near Spirit Mountain

Background, Newberry Mountains

The distinctive layering is still visible in places such as Loaf Rock just north of Katherine Landing.

Starting with the Pyramid Mine in the mid 1800s, the Katherine-Union Pass area became a booming mining district. Things took off even more with teamster S. C. Baggs's discovery in 1900 of a gold claim that became the Catherine (later Katherine) Mine. For the next thirty years, towns and mines and mills flourished. Most closed during the

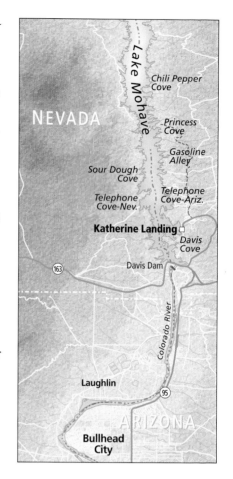

Davis Dam

Depression, except the Katherine Mine, which ran contin-
uously until 1943.

Lake Mohave Resort at Katherine Landing, located
on the east side just above Davis Dam, is the only full-
service marina in this part of the lake.

South of Katherine, an impoundment has been created in Davis Cove as a "grow out" area for young razorback suckers. Here the juvenile fish are sheltered to avoid
predation by non-native fish so they can reach adulthood.

Davis Dam, spanning Pyramid Canyon, marks the
beginning—and the end—of Lake Mohave adventures.
Here the booming tourism industry in Laughlin, Nevada,
and its sister town, Bullhead City, Arizona, is very much in
evidence, contributing to a rapid increase in visitors to the
lower end of Lake Mohave, especially the Katherine area.